# prayer

# Communicating with God

Neighborhood Bible Study Publishers
Dobbs Ferry, New York

# Communicating with God

neighborhood bible studies

12 Discussions for Group Bible Study
Carol Wilson

Scripture quotations, unless otherwise indicated, are taken from the HOLY BIBLE, NEW INTERNATIONAL VERSION®. Copyright © 1973, 1978, 1984 by International Bible Society. Used by permission of Zondervan Publishing House. All rights reserved.

Scripture quotations from THE MESSAGE. Copyright © 1995, 1994, 1995. Used by permission of NavPress Publishing Group.

All rights reserved. No part of this book may be reproduced or transmitted in any form or by any means, electronic or mechanical, including photocopying, recording, or any information storage and retrieval system without written permission from Neighborhood Bible Studies, 56 Main Street, Dobbs Ferry, New York, 10522.

Copyright ©1998 by Carol Wilson

ISBN 1-880266-30-X
Second Printing 2001
Printed in the United States of America
Cover by Tom Greene

## CONTENTS

How To Use This Discussion Guide . . . . . . . . . . . . . . . . . . . . . . 7

Introduction . . . . . . . . . . . . . . . . . . . . . . . . . . . . . . . . . . . . . . 11

**Discussion 1**  **Psalms 42; 43**
*Pursuit of Prayer; Thirst for God* . . . . . . . . . 13

**Discussion 2**  **Luke 11:1-10; John 16:23, 24**
*Privilege of Prayer; The Invitation* . . . . . . . . . 19

**Discussion 3**  **Matthew 6:9-13**
*Pattern for Prayer; The Lord's Prayer* . . . . . . 27

**Discussion 4**  **Psalm 145; 1 Chronicles 29:10-20**
*The Power of Praise;*
*Hallowed Be Your Name* . . . . . . . . . . . . . . . 33

**Discussion 5**  **Psalm 67; Colossians 4:2-6;**
**2 Thessalonians 3:1, 2**
*Purpose of Prayer; Your Kingdom Come* . . . 39

**Discussion 6**  **Psalm 37:1-9; John 15:5-16**
*Attitude of Prayer; Your Will Be Done* . . . . . 45

**Discussion 7**  **Matthew 6:19-34; 7:7-12**
*Praying for Daily Needs;*
*Give Us Today Our Daily Bread* . . . . . . . . . . 51

| Discussion 8 | 1 John 1:5-10; Psalm 51:1-17; Matthew 18:21-35 *Asking and Granting Forgiveness; Forgive Us Our Debts* ................... **57** |
|---|---|
| Discussion 9 | James 1:13-15; 4:6-10; Ephesians 6:10-20 *Praying for Deliverance; Deliver Us from the Evil One* ............ **63** |
| Discussion 10 | Nehemiah 1—13 *A Picture of Prayer in Real Life; The Book of Nehemiah* ................. **69** |
| Discussion 11 | Revelation 4:8-11; Colossians 1:15-20; 3:1-17 *Praying God's Words in Worship, Praise, and Confession* ................. **76** |
| Discussion 12 | Colossians 1:9-14; Romans 12:9-21 *Praying God's Words in Intercession and Petition* ................ **82** |

What Should Our Group Study Next? ................... **87**

## How to Use This Discussion Guide

This study guide uses the inductive approach to Bible study. *It will help you discover for yourself what the Bible says*. It will not give you prepackaged answers. *People remember most what they discover for themselves and what they express in their own words*. The study guide provides three kinds of questions:

1. What does the passage say? What are the facts?

2. What is the meaning of these facts?

3. How does this passage apply to your life?

Observe the facts carefully before you interpret the meaning of your observations. Then apply the truths you have discovered to life today. Resist the temptation to skip the fact questions since we are not as observant as we think. Find the facts quickly so you can spend more time on their meaning and application.

*The purpose of Bible study is not just to know more Bible truths but to apply them*. Allow these truths to make a difference in how you think and act, in your attitudes and relationships, in the quality and direction of your life.

Each discussion requires about one hour. Decide on the amount of time to add for socializing and prayer.

*Share the leadership*. If a different person is the moderator or question-asker each week, interest grows and members feel the group belongs to everyone. The Bible is the authority in the group, not the question-asker.

When a group grows to more than ten, the quiet people become quieter. Plan to grow and multiply. You can meet as two groups in the same house or begin another group so that more people can participate and benefit.

## Tools for an Effective Bible Study

1.  A study guide for each person in the group.

2.  A modern translation of the Bible such as:
    New International Version (NIV)
    Contemporary English Version (CEV)
    Jerusalem Bible (JB)
    New American Standard Bible (NASB)
    Revised English Bible (REB)
    New Revised Standard Version (NRSV)

3.  An English dictionary.

4.  A map of the Lands of the Bible in a Bible.

5.  Your conviction that the Bible is worth studying.


## Guidelines for Effective Study

1.  Stick to the passages under discussion.

2.  Avoid tangents. If the subject is not addressed in the passage, discuss it after the study.

3.  Let the Bible speak for itself. Do not quote other authorities or rewrite it to say what you want it to say.

4.  Apply the passage personally and honestly.

5.  Listen to one another to sharpen your insights.

6.  Prepare by reading the Bible passages and thinking through the questions during the week.

7.  Begin and end on time.

## Helps for the Question-Asker

1. Prepare by reading each study passage several times, using different translations if possible. Ask for God's help in understanding it. Consider how the questions might be answered. Observe which questions can be answered quickly and which may require more time.

2. Begin on time.

3. Lead the group in opening prayer or ask someone ahead of time to do so. Don't take anyone by surprise.

4. Ask for a different volunteer to read each Bible section. Read the question. Wait for an answer. Rephrase the question if necessary. Skip questions already answered by the discussion. Resist the temptation to answer the question yourself.

5. Encourage everyone to participate. Ask the group, "What do the rest of you think?" "What else could be added?"

6. Receive all answers warmly. If needed, ask, "In which verse did you find that?" "How does that fit with verse...?"

7. If a tangent arises, ask, "Do we find the answer to that here?" Or suggest, "Let's write that down and look for the information as we go along."

8. Discourage members who are too talkative by saying, "When I read the next question, let's hear from someone who hasn't spoken yet today."

9. Close the study using one or more of the *practicing prayer* suggestions.

10. Decide on one person to be the host and another person to be the question-asker for the next discussion.

## INTRODUCTION

Libraries and bookstores have whole shelves filled with books about prayer. This study guide acknowledges its debt to all the good books that have already been written.

In the first study, we explore our secret longings and discover how prayer brings us to the One who satisfies those deep desires. Then, because we are followers of Jesus Christ, we immerse ourselves in eight studies of the prayer Jesus gave us. We search for practical ways to apply Jesus' pattern to our praying and living. The last three studies introduce ways to use God's words in the Bible to shape our prayers. In every study, the section *Practicing Prayer* gives you an opportunity to immediately begin using what you are learning.

When you finish this study, you may have more questions about prayer than you have now. You may not understand how prayer "works." You probably won't understand why sometimes prayer doesn't seem to work. And you probably won't be able to pass a seminary examination on the subject of prayer.

But what I hope you'll do is pray! Healthy communication reflects a healthy relationship. As you discover more about God and how eager he is to be your friend, may you find a growing delight in talking with him. This study is designed to help you want to pray, dare to pray and to pray.

## *A Personal Testimony*

I have several compelling reasons to meet with God each day:

- God's desire for my fellowship and worship
- the example of Jesus and all my Christian heroes
- fascination with the Bible
- many concerns to bring to God
- my inability to live for God without his help

But for me, the strongest call to time with God is my personal need for those moments with him. It is in the quiet place with God that the loose strands and ragged edges of my life are brought back to wholeness. It is there that I learn daily to seek God's point of view about things. Other voices clamor loudly throughout the day, each telling its own lie about my worth, my purpose, my obligations, my flaws and my destiny. But when I'm with God, he restores my soul. He seats me in my rightful place with Christ in the spiritual realm and shows me his perspective. God reminds me that Jesus is everything: his work on the cross, his victory, his glory—these are the essentials of life. I need to see that every day.

-Carol Wilson

## DISCUSSION 1

# The Pursuit of Prayer; Thirst for God

*Psalms 42; 43*

A sense of guilt or duty might motivate someone to do a good thing for awhile, but not for a lifetime. Whether learning a language or exercising regularly or caring unselfishly for a loved one or praying, you need a strong desire in the core of your being to keep you going.

*Read Psalm 42:1-4*

1. From verse 1, picture a deer being chased over hills, through woods and across fields by hunters or a pack of dogs. Describe its physical symptoms and the intensity of its thirst.

2. Describe the intensity of the psalmist's thirst for God.

3. What are some of the circumstances of life today that could cause you to "eat tears" day and night?

4. What are some of the ways people in today's society try to quench their desperate inner thirst?

   How does the psalmist intend to satisfy his panting thirst?

5. Put yourself inside the skin of the psalmist and suggest other word pictures to describe that level of spiritual thirst.

*Read Psalms 42 and 43, noticing all the questions.*

*Note: Scholars generally agree that these verses were originally written as one prayer-poem, and were later split into two psalms.*

6. Record all the questions in these psalms, with verse references, on the following chart.

| Questions the psalmist's enemies ask him | Questions the psalmist asks God | Questions the psalmist asks himself |
|---|---|---|
|  |  |  |

7. Which question, mentioned twice, does the enemy ask over and over, all day long?

   Satan is the enemy of your soul. He may taunt you all day long with thoughts that seem like your own. When he raises the question, "Where is your God?" what are some possible responses you can make?

8. How does this repeated question affect the psalmist?

   How does it affect you?

9. What reasons might lie behind the questions the psalmist asks God?

   When have you felt like asking the same question?

*Note: On the cross, Jesus asked,"**My God, my God, why have you forsaken me?**" (Matthew 27:46).*

10. What basic truths about God does the psalmist cling to in these two psalms, even in his despair?

11. What questions does the psalmist ask of himself three times?

*Prayer*

What value might there be in asking this "Why?" question of yourself?

12. As the psalmist keeps asking himself why he's so *thirsty*, so *downcast*, so *disturbed*, what good advice does he give himself (verses 42:5, 11; 43:5)?

    How does he show that he expects to find satisfaction for his desperate thirst?

13. Psalm 42:8 stands at the very center, the pinnacle of this combined prayer-poem. How does this confident statement answer the devastating "Where?" question you looked at earlier?

14. Read 43:3, 4 aloud. What methods or means might God use to answer this prayer for you?

    Why would these verses be an excellent prayer to offer to God daily?

## Practicing Prayer

1. Using a word picture from question 5, tell God of your spiritual thirst for him, either silently or aloud. Ask God to teach you to draw closer and closer to him through prayer.

2. In Psalm 42:8, the psalmist affirms God's song in the night. In 43:4 he promises to praise God musically with the harp. Music is a meaningful channel for expressing prayer and praise to God. Use music this week to praise God. You might listen to Christian music, sing a favorite hymn, or make a special effort to sing with meaning and feeling in church. Plan to share with the group next time how you praised God musically.

3. If you are dissatisfied with the intensity of your desire for fellowship with God, what could you do this week to help that desire grow stronger?

## A Lesson from Nature

When a mother bird alights on the edge of the nest, it's the nestling with the loudest cry and the widest mouth that gets the food. God promises, ***Open your mouth wide, and I will fill it.*** *

\* Psalm 81:10 RSV

*Prayer*

## DISCUSSION 2

# The Privilege of Prayer; The Invitation

*Luke 11:1-10; John 16:23, 24*

Think of the difference between crashing a party where you hope no one evicts you and being the guest of honor where you're invited and wanted. How wonderful to come to God in prayer knowing you're wanted, that God himself invites you to pray!

In the preceding study we saw how important it is to feel, acknowledge and feed our deep desire for personal contact with God. The psalmist likened his desire for fellowship with God to the desperate thirst of a fleeing deer. The greater our desire, the more faithfully we will pray. And the more we pray, the more our desire for God increases.

But our fellowship with God doesn't depend primarily on us. God himself is eager for us to pray; he invites us, and gives us the privilege of talking with him. As proof of God's invitation to us, we will consider some of the statements of the Lord Jesus himself.

In this study, we'll examine the prayer Jesus gave on two different occasions. It is historically called "the Lord's prayer," but it is equally appropriate to call it "the Christian's model prayer."

## *Model for Prayer*
*Read Luke 11:1-4*

1. How has your desire for prayer increased since you met for the last study?


2. What do Jesus' followers observe that stirs up their desire to know how to pray?

   What evidence do you see here that Jesus is pleased with their request?


3. How does Jesus say one should address God in beginning a prayer?

   What does that title imply about your relationship with God?


4. Luke 10:21 records a brief prayer by Jesus. How does he address God?

   How could you ever be so bold as to use the same approach?

5. Read the prayer in several translations. Make a list of the different things Jesus tells us to pray for.

*Note: Here is a contemporary version:*
> **Father, reveal who you are. Set the world right.**
> **Keep us alive with three square meals.**
> **Keep us forgiven with you and forgiving others.**
> **Keep us safe from ourselves and the Devil.**
> —Eugene Peterson, *THE MESSAGE*

6. In your current personal circumstances, which need comes first to your mind?

   In which section of the model prayer does your request fit best?

## Motivation for Prayer

Without even saying "Amen," Jesus moves on to tell a story intended to motivate us to pray.

*Read Luke 11:5-10.*

7. Give all the information you find about the three characters in Jesus' story:

   the one with a need

   the one with resources

   the one in the middle

8. Picture yourself as *the person in the middle* as you pray. Who is represented by *the one with the resources* to meet needs?

   Whom do you know that is represented by *the person with needs*?

*Note: Jesus' stories were based on real-life situations. An event like this one likely occurred repeatedly in that era in the Middle East. Not every detail of an illustrative story can be applied directly. For example, while the friend in the story was reluctant to help because of his own comfort, we cannot ascribe that same motive to the Friend to whom we bring our requests in prayer on behalf of our needy friends.*

### Principles for Prayer

9. The petitioner forms a link between two of his friends. What does his behavior tell you about his feelings towards those two friends?

10. How does Jesus characterize this petitioner's pleading (verse 8)?

11. What principles for effectively praying for others can you learn from "the friend in the middle" in this story?

    What changes could you make in your prayer life to follow these principles?

12. What response does Jesus promise to this kind of praying?

13. In your own words, summarize the promises given in verses 9 and 10.

*Note: the Greek word translated **ask** also means **beg.***

*Read John 16:23, 24*

14. John 14—16 recounts Jesus' last night with his disciples before his death. He shocks them with bad news of his leaving, but comforts them with promises. Summarize Jesus' promise and the condition regarding prayer in John 16:23, 24.

| Promise | Condition |
|---------|-----------|
|         |           |

*Note: In the Bible, often one's **name** carries the identity of the person's nature and character. Asking "in Jesus' name" is not a magical formula; it means asking according to who he is and what he desires. It's like a blank check you present to the Bank of Heaven. You and Jesus are the co-signers. You wouldn't fill the blank line with a request that Jesus wouldn't be happy to co-sign.*

15. Matthew 18:19, 20 says, "*I tell you that if two of you on earth agree about anything you ask for, it will be done for you by my Father in heaven. For where two or three come together in my name, there am I with them.*" How many are in your group at this moment?

    How many visible?

    How many invisible?

## Practicing Prayer

1. In silent prayer, tell Jesus how glad you are that he is present with you.

2. Go back to question 6 and think about what you'd like Jesus to do regarding that need. You may wish to write down your request in one or two sentences.

3. After everyone has had time to think and write, take turns telling your concerns aloud to the Lord who is present in your group. Ask for his help. By faith, say thanks for his presence, his promise, and for what he will do.

*As you close, pray together:*

> *Father,*
> *hallowed be your name,*
> *your kingdom come.*
> *Give us each day our daily bread.*
> *Forgive us our sins,*
> *for we also forgive everyone who sins against us.*
> *And lead us not into temptation.*
> *Amen.*

*Prayer*

## DISCUSSION 3

# Pattern for Prayer; The Lord's Prayer

*Matthew 6:9-13*

In the preceding study, we saw how eager God is for us to pray to him. Jesus himself (1) invites us to pray, (2) promises our prayers will be heard and answered, (3) models prayer, and (4) gives us an outline for our prayers. In Luke 11, Jesus gave the prayer in response to his disciples who saw him praying and asked, "***Lord, teach us to pray.***" The similar prayer in today's study was given as part of Jesus' Sermon on the Mount recorded in Matthew 5—7.

> Jesus declares, "***Your Father knows what you need.***" Matthew 6:8
> *Then what can I tell him?*
> Human logic says: "Nothing!"
> Jesus says: "Anything!"

*Read Matthew 6:9-13*

1. Why do you think Jesus gave the same pattern for prayer in both Luke 11 and Matthew 6?

In today's study you will identify the various sections of this model prayer to provide a guide for praying effectively according to Jesus' pattern.

## Drawing Near - Our Father in heaven

2. Jesus is addressing his disciples and a crowd of listeners. How does he tell you to begin your prayer?

3. What is the significance of the first word in the prayer?

   Why does he use **our, we** and **us** throughout the prayer?

4. When you say *Father in heaven*, what does it do for your perspective?

## Worship - Hallowed be your name

*Note: In the Bible, and also in the culture of that day, a name was not merely a means of identifying the person or getting his/her attention. A person's name carried the full weight of his/her character, abilities and commitments.*

5. As a group, read aloud *Hallowed be your name*.

   How does your dictionary define *hallowed*?

*Pattern for Prayer; The Lord's Prayer*

What is Jesus suggesting that his followers should desire in praying these words?


6. One way to hallow the Lord's name is to use the words of the Bible as your prayer. Assign one person in the group to read the first two verses of Psalm 95, the next, to read verses 1 and 2 of Psalm 96, and so on, through Psalm 100.

   Now, using your own words, offer a sentence of worship to God.

## Mission - Your kingdom come

7. What is Jesus urging his followers to long and pray for in verse 10a, ***Your kingdom come***?

   When the kingdom of God comes, what difference do you think it will make in the world?

   What changes would you predict in the life of a person, family, or community where Jesus is made king?

8. What present situation in your life needs to be brought under the kingship of Jesus right now?

## Submission - Your will be done

9. Jesus modeled submission as he faced crucifixion, praying "*My Father, if it is possible, may this cup be taken from me. Yet not as I will, but as you will*" (Matthew 26:39).

   Why is it important to have this attitude when you bring your requests to God?

## Petition - Give us today our daily bread

10. What does the request in 6:11 tell you about Jesus' attitude towards the physical and material needs of his children?

## Practicing Prayer

Think about the physical and material needs of others and yourself, remembering that Jesus teaches us to say *us* and *our* rather than *me* and *my*. Ask God to meet those needs.

## Pardon - Forgive . . . as we also have forgiven

11. What petition does Jesus urge us to make in verse 12?

What is the attitude of a person who sincerely asks for forgiveness?

*Note: **Debts,** used in some translations, refers to moral offenses.*

13. Compare Luke 18:9-14 with verse 12. How does Jesus view the two characters in this passage?

From their outward behavior, which of the two men in this story would you rather have as a neighbor?

Why doesn't God forgive the Pharisee?

*Note: **As we also have forgiven our debtors** may be the hardest thing you'll ever have to say. A future study will deal with this transaction in greater depth.*

### Spiritual Warfare - Lead us not into temptation but deliver us from the evil one

13. Following the focus on forgiveness, what does Jesus teach that one should pray (verse 13)?

14. What does this request reveal about God?

about ourselves?

*Note:* **Deliver us from the evil one** brings up the subject of the enemy of our souls, the devil. In a later study we'll consider what he's up to, how he works, and how we can resist him.

## Practicing Prayer

1. Although the oldest manuscripts do not include a closing word of thanks and praise, for centuries Christians have offered a beautiful blessing to God at the end of this model prayer. Read it together as a prayer.

    *For yours is the kingdom*
    *and the power*
    *and the glory forever.*
    *Amen.*

2. Jesus promises that where two or more gather in his name, he will be present. So Jesus himself is there *with* you as a member of your group. Several people may want to voice their thanks to him for this model prayer, and for what you have learned today.

## DISCUSSION 4

# The Power of Praise; Hallowed Be Your Name

*Psalm 145; 1 Chronicles 29:10-20*

After an excellent musical performance, we applaud. When an athlete makes a spectacular catch, we shout and cheer. In the presence of a splendid natural wonder, we gaze silently in awe and amazement. If we find an unusually good book or bakery or perennial plant, we tell our friends. And when we reflect on who God is and what he is like, we praise him.

Jesus' model prayer (Matthew 6:9-13) begins with ***"Our Father in heaven, hallowed be your name."*** The dictionary defines *hallowed* as sacred, holy and highly honored. Since God is infinitely worthy of this honor, it gives him pleasure when we acknowledge his worth.

In addition to giving God pleasure, what benefit might you get out of beginning your prayer in this way?

*Read Psalm 145:1, 2, 21*

1. How do these verses, which open and close this praise/prayer, relate to the opening words of Jesus' model prayer?

    Psalm 145 contains four poetic paragraphs that more fully hallow the name of God. Let the repetition, which is typical of Hebrew poetry, serve as a reminder to you rather than a distraction.

## His Mighty Acts
*Read Psalm 145:3-7*

2. What aspects of God's character does the writer celebrate in this paragraph?

3. When people are in unstructured social settings, conversations often revolve around their heroes, whether athletes, entertainers, entrepreneurs, great thinkers, etc. According to verse 4, who is the hero worth bragging about?

    How did the generation before you commend the LORD to you?

4. How could you apply verse 4 in your relationship with a younger person in your home, neighborhood, workplace or church?

## His Grace and Compassion
*Read Psalm 145:8-13a*

5. What qualities of God's character do you find in verses 8 and 9?

   Select at least one of those traits and tell why, at this point in your life, it's important to you to be able to pray to a God like that.

6. In verse 12, what is the result of God's people faithfully telling about his wonderful qualities?

## His Faithfulness
*Read Psalm 145:13b-16*

7. Who are the beneficiaries of God's faithfulness as specifically described in these verses?

8. Which of these verses are especially meaningful to you, and why?

9. How can we reconcile the ideal of God's loving plan with the realities of our fallen world?

## His Righteousness
### Read Psalm 145:17-20

10. What does it mean to you to worship a God who is righteous, who always does what is right, good and just?

11. Each of the four verses in this section gives a different description of those who are the recipients of God's goodness. Summarize them:

| Verse | Recipients | What God does for them |
|-------|------------|------------------------|
| 17    |            |                        |
| 18    |            |                        |
| 19    |            |                        |
| 20    |            |                        |

How can you as a worshiper relate to this?

12. What other side of God's righteousness is shown in the last line of verse 20?

13. Psalm 145:8 may remind you of the line in the Lord's Prayer, **Forgive us our debts**. What other statements in this psalm relate to different sections of the Lord's Prayer?

*Note: Psalm 145 was written by David, king of Israel. Despite his failings, he was one of the few kings who kept his heart turned toward God until he died. David longed to build a temple for corporate worship, but God told him his son Solomon was the one he had chosen for the task. Disappointed but undaunted, David proceeded in his old age to gather all the building materials his son would need. Then David called all the people together to celebrate.*

### Read 1 Chronicles 29:14-20

14. How does David describe himself in this prayer?

    How does he describe his people?

15. What is David's view of the materials he and the people have donated?

16. What does David ask God to do for his people and for Solomon?

*Note: David's confessions and petitions follow one of the most splendid hymns of praise in all of Scripture, verses 10-13.*

## Practicing Prayer

1. Take turns reading aloud the lines of this praise prayer, 1 Chronicles 29:10-13:

   *Praise be to you, O LORD, God of our father Israel,*
   *from everlasting to everlasting.*

   *Yours, O LORD, is the greatness and the power*
   *and the glory and the majesty and the splendor,*
   *for everything in heaven and earth is yours.*

   *Yours, O LORD, is the kingdom;*
   *you are exalted as head over all.*

   *Wealth and honor come from you;*
   *you are the ruler of all things.*

   *In your hands are strength and power*
   *to exalt and give strength to all.*

   *Now, our God, we give you thanks,*
   *and praise your glorious name.*

2. In your own words, hallow God's name by telling God something you appreciate about him.

## DISCUSSION 5

# The Purpose of Prayer; Your Kingdom Come

*Psalm 67; Colossians 4:2-6; 2 Thessalonians 3:1, 2*

A minister once asked a group of children, "What is prayer?" A young boy answered, "Prayer is what you do when there's no other way to get what you want." A better definition would be, "Prayer is God's way of giving us what he wants." In our wildest dreams we can't imagine how wonderful life would be if we were, as God intended, obedient citizens of his kingdom of love. That's what God wants! But it is obvious that his beautiful plan has been marred by sin. So we say, "Your kingdom come," praying that around the world people will come to know God, love him and let him be king in their lives.

### Your Kingdom Come
*Read Psalm 67:1-7*

1. What do these worshipers want for themselves (verses 1, 6, 7)?

2. How are the things these worshipers want for themselves linked with what God wants to do for all the nations of the world (verse 2-5)?

3. What kind of king is God, and what are the conditions in his kingdom (verse 4)?

4. Why do you think there are still billions of people who don't know God's ways or his salvation?

5. What prayers could you offer that would go along with the request *your kingdom come?*

## *Praying Practical Prayers*
*Read Colossians 4:2-6*

Paul writes this book from Rome where he's a prisoner because of powerful opposition to his missionary work. He obviously continues his mission work despite his imprisonment.

6. What three qualities of prayer does Paul urge his readers to practice (verse 2)?

   How can you apply these three qualities in a practical way?

7. What are the two prayer requests this missionary sends to his praying friends (verses 3, 4)?

8. This passage describes a three-way partnership between the senders, the missionaries, and God. What is the role of each one?

9. What country or region of the world do you know that is closed to the message of Jesus?

   What impact could your prayers, patterned after verses 3 and 4, have on people there?

10. What evidence do you see in verses 5 and 6 that the missionaries are not just needed *out there* in foreign countries?

11. This passage implies that our lives need to be consistent with our prayers. What changes would you like God to make in you so you could better fulfill verses 5 and 6?

## Praying for Missionaries
### Read 2 Thessalonians 3:1, 2

12. What prayer requests is Paul, the missionary, making for himself?

13. Picture a missionary being sent by God to a group of people who have never yet heard of Jesus and his love. If you were that missionary, how important would it be to you to have friends back home praying these prayers for you?

14. At the beginning of this study, prayer was defined as "God's way of giving us what he wants." How do these prayer requests in Colossians and 2 Thessalonians relate to what God wants, i.e., his kingdom?

## Practicing Prayer

1. Pray for one another based on the requests mentioned in Question 11.

2. Pray for a friend, relative or neighbor who needs to know God.

3. Choose one of Paul's prayer requests and pray it for a missionary you know or for a country or ethnic group that needs to hear about Jesus.

4. Practice the habit of praying *Your kingdom come.*

*Prayer*

## DISCUSSION 6

# Attitude of Prayer; Your Will Be Done

*Psalm 37:1-9; John 15:5-16*

Most of us have been disappointed by not getting what we prayed for. Perhaps someone told you that your problem was that you didn't have enough faith. God's promises to answer prayer are so sweeping that we might assume we just need to decide what we want and we'll get it. How can we reconcile those promises with our unanswered prayer? Jesus' model prayer indicates that submission to God is a prerequisite for praying God's way. *Your will be done on earth as it is in heaven.*

## The Right Attitude
*Read Psalm 37:1-9*

1. One of life's big riddles is why bad things happen to good people. Even more puzzling perhaps is why good things happen to bad people. It might seem as if God is answering their prayers. What does the psalmist David urge his people not to be anxious about (verses 1, 7)?

   What reasons does he give in verses 2, 8 and 9?

2. In verse 4, what is the key to receiving your heart's desires?

   What does this imply about a person's values and priorities?

   If you live according to the first half of verse 4, how might it affect your heart's desires?

3. What positive steps does the psalmist command or recommend in verses 1-9?

   What two or three attitudes best summarize all these commands?

## *Essential Relationship*
## *Read John 15:5-8*

*Note: This is part of Jesus' final message to his disciples before he was taken away to be crucified. Jesus considered it essential information!*

4. Draw a picture, either on paper or with words, to describe the relationship Jesus invites us to have with him (verse 5).

   What warning is here for those who do not have such a relationship with Jesus?

5. In this picture from nature, what is the inevitable product of a healthy plant?

   Why can't a branch produce fruit by itself?

6. In the spiritual realm, why can't a person produce fruit apart from Jesus and his word?

   What qualities will be seen in a person who is bearing much fruit?

7. What does Jesus promise here about prayer?

   What is the connection between Jesus' words and prayer according to verse 7?

8. In the picture you drew of the relationship in question 4, where would you place yourself?

   If you're not satisfied in that position, what will you do about it?

*Read John 15:9-16*

9. Jesus tells us to pray *your will be done on earth.* In John 15 he shows us how this attitude of commitment works out in our daily lives. What

behaviors and attitudes are God's will according to verses 9-15?

10. Picture an organizational chart of a family business from the metaphor in verse 15. Include everyone mentioned: Master (Father), Son, friends, and servants.

   Where do you place yourself in the chart?

11. What, according to Jesus, is the difference between friends and servants?

   How can a person today gain access to the truth Jesus makes known to his friends?

12. How should knowing God's will affect a person's prayers?

13. What promise about prayer does Jesus make in verse 16?

   How is asking in someone's name like asking according to their will?

*Attitude of Prayer; Your Will Be Done*

14. Summarize the conditions for the promises in this passage.

    What practical steps can you take to meet those conditions?

To say *your will be done* involves yielding to God's will. To pray *according to his will* requires knowledge of what God is up to in his "family business." The better we know God's Word, the more we know what his will is. When we pray according to his will, we can be confident he will answer.

## Practicing Prayer

*If you drop a pebble into water, the ripples move outward in ever-widening circles. This is a good picture of the way our prayers can move out from our most personal concerns to the remotest places on earth. Since God is everywhere, he is equally concerned with everyone in all those widening circles.*

Pray for God's will to be done in specific situations in:

- *your personal life or family.*

- *your community:* neighborhood, workplace, city, schools, churches, local government, etc.

*As you move out to broader circles, your newspapers, radio and television will alert you to issues needing prayer.*

- *your nation:* president, elected representatives, judges, military personnel, and national trends that affect people's views of life and God.

- *the world:* people suffering from calamities currently in the news; churches and believers faithfully reflecting God within their culture; those taking the gospel to people who have not yet had a chance to hear it.

***Your will be done on earth as it is in heaven. Amen.***

*DISCUSSION 7*

# Praying for Daily Needs; Give Us Today Our Daily Bread

*Matthew 6:19-34; 7:7-12*

Some people might feel that God is too great or preoccupied to be bothered with their small concerns. The Bible invites you to *cast all your anxiety on him because he cares for you* (1 Peter 5:7). There is nothing you and your loved ones need that he is indifferent to, or cannot provide. Let the request for daily bread in Jesus' model prayer represent all your own material and physical needs, as well as those of others you care about.

*Balanced or Burdened?*
*Read Matthew 6:9-13*

1. Of all the requests in the Lord's prayer, how many relate to physical needs?

   How does your personal prayer life compare to the balance between material and spiritual requests as modeled here?

*Read Matthew 6:19-24*

2. What warnings does Jesus give here about the dangers of loving material things too much?

*Trusting or Worrying*
*Read Matthew 6:25-34*

3. How does Jesus' teaching here regarding ***daily bread*** relate to the previous phrase ***your will be done***?

4. How do people usually handle these concerns that Jesus tells us not to worry about?

5. As the cure for worry, examine the facts Jesus gives us about God.

| What does God do? | What does God know? | How does God view you? |
|---|---|---|
|  |  |  |

6. In this passage, Jesus makes his point with a series of questions. List the questions and give the obvious answers.

7. Jesus does not say that our material needs are unimportant. How does the promise in verse 33 assure you that your material needs are important to God?

What does it mean for a person to *seek first his kingdom*?

8. The final sentence could be depressing if read by itself. What attitude have you learned in this passage that will help you not to worry about your tomorrows?

## *Asking and Receiving*
*Read Matthew 7:7-12*

*Note: The commands in verse 7 in the original Greek are in the verb tense that implies continual, not one-time, action: Keep on doing it.*

9. Summarize Jesus' promises in verses 7 and 8.

What progression do you see from *asking* to *seeking* and from *seeking* to *knocking*?

10. From verses 9-11, describe a normal parent's response to his/her child's request.

What would you conclude about the parent who substituted a dangerous look-alike for the good thing the child requested?*

What effect would such a substitution have on the child's relationship with the parent?

*Note: Tragically, such abuse does occur in some dysfunctional homes. Victims of evil or irresponsible parents find healing in trusting their heavenly Father.*

11. What is the wonderful, obvious conclusion about prayer in verse 11?

    This is the third use of the words **much more** in today's Scripture (6:26, 30; 7:11). What do these words tell you about God's attitude towards you?

12. If by chance the child in verses 9 and 10 asks for a dangerous look-alike rather than a good thing, how will a normal parent answer that request?

    How will the heavenly Father respond if his child asks for something that looks good but isn't?

13. What attitude towards God do you want to have when it appears God isn't answering your prayers?

14. Verse 12 is well known as the Golden Rule for ethical behavior. Yet it is obviously part of this paragraph on prayer. Jesus must intend that we apply the Golden Rule to our prayers of petition. What kinds of praying would violate the Golden Rule?

## Practicing Prayer

### Read Philippians 4:6,7

1. With confidence based on what you've studied today, talk to God about the ***daily bread*** you and others need. After one person voices a request, let someone else in the group ask God to grant the request. Don't forget to thank him, by faith, for the coming answer.

2. On a piece of paper, write your name and a need you're asking God to meet. Let each member of the group take home someone else's prayer request to pray for daily until your next meeting.

3. Close with a prayer of thanks for prayers God has already answered. Thank him that his peace will guard your hearts and minds in Christ Jesus, as promised in Philippians 4:7.

*Prayer*

## DISCUSSION 8

# Asking and Granting Forgiveness; Forgive Us Our Debts

*1 John 1:5-10; Psalm 51:1-17; Matthew 18:21-35*

Why doesn't God answer prayer? Sometimes it is because we are asking for the wrong thing. Other times it is because of unforgiven sin. The Bible says, ***If I had cherished sin in my heart, the Lord would not have listened*** (Psalm 66:18). That's why Jesus included ***forgive us our debts*** (Matthew 6:12) in the pattern for prayer that he gave us. He knows us better than we know ourselves. Jesus knows we will do wrong things daily, and he knows that only those whose sins are forgiven can come confidently to the Father in prayer.

Another hindrance to prayer is our failure to forgive others. That's why Jesus continued, ***...as we also have forgiven our debtors***. Someone might say, "I've been hurt so badly I can never forgive." This is an all-too-common reality for many who have been deeply hurt. The second part of today's study grapples with this difficult statement in the Lord's prayer.

## Forgive Us Our Sins
## Read 1 John 1:5-10

1. How would you describe the behavior of a person who is walking *in the darkness*?

   How does this affect his/her relationship with God?

2. What is the condition of the person who is walking *in the light*?

3. What is the true condition of a person who claims to be perfect?

4. What is the solution for those who agree with God about their need for forgiveness and cleansing?

*Note: the word **confess** means to agree with. To confess sins is to name them and agree with God's view of them.*

5. Which is harder to do: agree with God when you have sinned, or pretend that nothing happened and everything is all right?

*Asking and Granting Forgiveness; Forgive Us Our Debts*

### Read Psalm 51:1-6

*Note: David prayed this prayer of repentance and confession after he became aware of his sin and guilt.*

6. What evidence do you see here that David agrees with God about his sin?

7. What characteristics of God does he appeal to?

### Read Psalm 51:10-17

8. From this passage, describe the attitude of a person who agrees with God about his sin.

9. What characteristics of God give you courage to confess your sins when you become aware of them?

What can you expect God to do in response?

## Practicing Prayer for Forgiveness

The psalmist knew he must recognize his sins before he could confess them. You can use his prayer: ***Search me, O God, and know my heart; test me and know my anxious thoughts. See if there is any offensive way in me, and lead me in the way everlasting*** (Psalm 139:23, 24). Take a few silent moments for members to search their inner beings for hidden sin, agree with God about it, and claim his forgiveness on the basis of the cleansing blood of Jesus.

After an appropriate time of silence, the leader may say "Amen" and move on to the next section.

### As We Also Have Forgiven Our Debtors

*Note: When Jesus finished giving his model prayer, without even saying "Amen" he went on to say,* ***For if you forgive men when they sin against you, your heavenly Father will also forgive you. But if you do not forgive men their sins, your Father will not forgive your sins*** *( Matthew 6:14, 15). Tough words!*

### Read Matthew 18:21, 22

10. Peter's question in verse 21 must have seemed extremely generous to him. Peter's reaction to Jesus' response isn't recorded. How would you have reacted if Jesus had said that to you?

### Read Matthew 18:23-35

*Note: Ten thousand talents would equal several million dollars and a hundred denarii would equal a few dollars.*

11. How does this story relate to Peter's question about forgiveness?

12. Imagine the emotions of the first servant when the king demands payment, when he begs for mercy, and when the king cancels the debt.

13. What attitude would you expect from someone who has just been forgiven a debt impossible to repay?

14. How does the king's judgment of the unforgiving servant reveal God's attitude toward a refusal to forgive another person (verses 32-35)?

15. Think of the people who have hurt you the most, who owe you the most. How do their debts to you compare with your debt to God?

*Note: This calculation is only in comparison to your debt to God. It is not intended to trivialize the extent of that person's offense against you, which may have been horrendous.*

## Practicing Prayers of Forgiveness

1. If you have much to forgive, you may find it helpful to take just the first step. Pray, "Lord, I'm willing for you to make me willing to forgive." Or despite the emotions you may be feeling, you may be ready to ask God to help you forgive those who have sinned against you. Let the rest of the group support you in prayer if forgiving is a difficult struggle for you right now.

2. This week, as memories of the pain you have suffered come back to your mind, remind yourself that God in mercy has forgiven you and you can forgive your debtor. Crowd out bitter and unforgiving thoughts by reading and meditating on Psalm 103.

3. Thank God for his grace and mercy in forgiving all your sins. As God makes you aware of your sins (of commission or omission, of thought, speech, or behavior), agree with him and ask his forgiveness. Thank him that *If we confess our sins, he is faithful and just and will forgive us our sins and purify us from all unrighteousness* (1 John 1:9).

> *Forgive us our debts, as we also have forgiven our debtors. Amen.*

## DISCUSSION 9

# Praying for Deliverance; Deliver Us from the Evil One

*James 1:13-15; 4:6-10; Ephesians 6:10-20*

Many man-made religions, both eastern and western, try to deny the existence or power of evil. Not Jesus! He teaches us to recognize the power of temptation and the evil one, and to withstand them both by prayer.

The Bible teaches that Satan, a created angel who was banished from heaven because of his pride and rebellion, is engaged in a cosmic struggle against God's person, God's purposes, and God's people. Satan is also called the devil, the evil one, the tempter, the serpent, etc. No wonder Jesus taught us to pray, *and lead us not into temptation, but deliver us from the evil one.*

### The Nature of Temptation
*Read James 1:13-15*

1. What is the source of temptation according to this passage?

2. What is it about temptation that is so enticing and potentially destructive?

3. Compare James 1:13 with Jesus' words, *lead us not into temptation*.

## Attitude for Overcoming
### Read James 4:6-10

4. Summarize the attitudes that are taught here:

   attitude towards God

   attitude towards yourself and your sin

   attitude towards the devil

5. If you follow the teaching of these verses, what will God do?

   What will the devil do?

6. In the past day or two, what opportunities have you had to put these attitudes into practice?

*Note: Many temptations arise solely from within a person's own sinful nature (the Bible calls this the flesh, Romans 8:13, NRSV). Other temptations come from the surrounding society (the Bible calls this the world, 1 John 2:16). Both the flesh and the world are in opposition to God because of the malicious work of God's enemy the devil (Satan). His quarrel is really with God, so it is God's battle and he has won the ultimate victory over Satan through Christ's death and resurrection. Still, as long as we're on earth, our lives are part of the battlefield on which Satan chooses to fight against God. We cannot escape this battle. But we can learn to fight the devil God's way.*

## *Equipment for Spiritual Battle*
### *Read Ephesians 6:10-19*

Keep in mind that Jesus, the commander, provides equipment for the fulfillment of *his* goals, not the soldier's goals.

7. How can you obey the command in verse 10?


8. To resist the enemy you need information about his strategies. What do you learn about the devil in Ephesians 6:11-16 and 2:1-3?


How do these descriptions motivate you to pray ***deliver us from the evil one***?


9. The *belt* (6:14a) was a strong leather girdle worn by Roman soldiers around their waist and hips. Their weapons were hung from it, and they tucked their skirts into it when they needed to move quickly.

What protection would ***the belt of truth*** provide in spiritual warfare?

How can you put on ***the belt of truth***?

10. The ***breastplate*** (verse 14b) protected the soldier's vital organs. The Christian's breastplate is righteousness. How can you put on the breastplate of righteousness? (See Titus 3:4-7.)

11. The soldier's *shoes* (verse 15) enabled him to advance over rough terrain. How can you use this spiritual equipment to advance the spread of the good news about Jesus?

12. Verse 16 makes it clear that the enemy will shoot flaming arrows at you. What might these arrows be that can be extinguished by ***the shield of faith***?

13. How does the ***helmet of salvation*** protect your mind (verse 17a)?

14. The ***sword of the Spirit*** is the only weapon listed for offense (verse 17b).

How do you take up the sword of the Spirit?

15. What have you learned in these studies on prayer that would help you obey the commands in verse 18?

## Practicing Prayer

1. God equips us for spiritual conflict so we can withstand Satan's attacks and participate in the victory of our commander, Jesus. How does Ephesians 6: 19, 20 relate to God's desire for the whole world to know him?

   Pray these requests in verses 19 and 20 for one another and for Christian workers who are in fear-producing situations.

2. James 4:7-10 encourages us to (1) draw near to God, (2) resist the devil, and (3) forsake our sin. How do the pieces of spiritual armor in Ephesians 6 relate to these attitudes?

   Pray together:

   > *Our Father in heaven, hallowed be your name, your kingdom come, your will be done on earth as it is in heaven. Give us today our daily bread. Forgive us our debts, as we also have forgiven our debtors. And lead us not into temptation, but deliver us from the evil one. Amen.*

*Prayer*

## DISCUSSION 10

# A Picture of Prayer in Real Life; The Book of Nehemiah

*Nehemiah 1—13*

The story of Nehemiah is actually a gallery of pictures of various kinds of prayer. Nehemiah is a displaced person far from his homeland, along with thousands of other Jews. They are descendants of the nation that was forcibly deported about 145 years earlier, following their defeat by the armies of Nebuchadnezzar, king of Babylon. Nehemiah has achieved a somewhat prominent position in the court of King Artaxerxes. But his personal identity is tied up with the nation of Israel, the people of God, many of whom have long since been allowed to return to the land of Israel. Now pick up the story.

*Read Nehemiah 1:1-4*

1. Describe the bad news Nehemiah receives about his people and their capital city.


2. What does Nehemiah's response to this bad news tell you about his emotions?

What kinds of bad news would it take to get you to respond like that?

## *Praying When You Have Time*
*Read Nehemiah 1:5-11*

3. This prayer seems to summarize several days of concentrated praying with fasting. Identify its components: worship, confession of sin, claiming God's promises, and intercession.

   Which of these elements of prayer do you include in your personal prayers?

   How could you add ones that are missing?

## *Praying When You Don't Have Time*
*Read Nehemiah 2:1-5*

4. Compare the time and setting for Nehemiah's prayer in this passage with that mentioned in 1:4.

*Note: In those days a civil servant risked death if he appeared before the king without a cheerful countenance.*

   How may the prayers referred to in 1:4-11 have laid a foundation for the quick, possibly silent, prayer referred to in 2:4?

5. What answers to Nehemiah's prayers do you see in 2:6-8, 12, 17-20?

## Praying When the Roof Caves In

6. Chapter 3 describes how various clans set to work to repair the wall nearest their homes. But in Chapter 4 the enemies of God and his people mount their opposition. Skim Chapter 4 and see how Nehemiah blends praying with working. What do you learn from this about the relationship between prayer and action?

Chapter 5 is an important lesson in integrity. Never mind praying well unless you also live honestly and justly. Read this chapter on your own sometime soon.

## Confessing Your Sin and
## Restoring Your Relationship with God
## Read Nehemiah 6:1-16

7. In Chapter 6, both the building and the opposition continue. What evidence do you see of Nehemiah's habit of prayer?

What is the good news in verses 15 and 16?

*Note: The battle isn't over. Now the people need to be restored. Chapters 7 and 8 tell about the restoration of the people. But when they hear the Law of the Lord read, they are devastated to realize how disobedient they had been.*

### Read Nehemiah 8:8-12

8. What instructions does Nehemiah give to the people?

   How would you list their reasons for joy in order of importance?

*Note: The remaining chapters of Nehemiah describe the spiritual restoration of the people, their renewal of their covenant with God, and the reinstatement of their spiritual leaders.*

9. What is the first step in their spiritual restoration (Nehemiah 8:18a)?

   What do they do next (Nehemiah 9:2-3)?

10. If you were leading a group of Christians in your community in a day of *solemn assembly* (8:18, NRSV), what are some of the sins being committed in your town and nation that you would want to confess on behalf of your people?

### Worshiping and Praising God Because He Is Worthy
*Skim Nehemiah 9 silently*

11. From the prayer the people pray together in 9:5-37, what examples of worship, confession, thanksgiving and petition do you find?

*A Picture of Prayer in Real Life; The Book of Nehemiah*

12. In a solemn assembly in your community, when it's time to lead in worship, what are some of the qualities of God for which you would worship him?

13. At last the wall is ready for its dedication, as described in Nehemiah 12:27-43. Skim these verses silently and slowly, letting your mind visualize the great drama and pageantry described here.

    How would you contrast the situation on this day with the situation at the beginning of the book?

14. What role has prayer played in this transformation?

## Practicing Prayer

1. Describe a time in your life when you, like Nehemiah:

    prayed when you had ample time

    prayed when you didn't have time

    prayed when the roof caved in

    confessed your sin and restored your relationship with God

    worshiped and praised God because he is worthy

2. What did you learn about prayer through that experience?

   What have you learned about God's response to prayer?

3. Nehemiah wept over the desperate situation of his people and Jerusalem, but he believed God could do the impossible. And Nehemiah had the joy of participating in the restoration of the people and the city.

4. Describe a circumstance that you know needs to be transformed by God. Pray together for those situations.

## DISCUSSION 11

# Praying God's Words in Worship, Praise, and Confession

*Revelation 4:8-11; Colossians 1:15-20; 3:1-17*

We could study prayer the rest of our lives and still feel inadequate to pray. It's important to remember that God our Father loves to hear from his children. He asks us to pray. It's also helpful to know that the Bible can guide our prayers. When you feel speechless in God's presence, you may find freedom in praying God's words back to him. These last two studies will explore some ways to let the Bible shape our prayers.

### Worship
*Read Revelation 4:8-11*

The first part of Revelation 4 contains a sincere attempt at an impossible task: to describe in human words the sights, sounds and sensations of heaven. Heaven defies description. It is fascinating to speculate on the meaning of all the symbols, but it's not within the scope of this study to explain all its mysteries. In verse 8, the focus shifts to God, the center of attraction in heaven.

1. What qualities of God do the living creatures focus on in their worship (verse 8)?

2. Why is it important that God is holy?

   That he is the Lord God Almighty?

   That he was, and is, and is to come?

3. What do verses 9-11 emphasize about God?

4. Why is God worthy to receive the worship described in these verses?

## Practicing Prayers of Worship

Sit silently for a few moments, reflecting on God's worth and how you feel towards him. Then worship him aloud, using words or concepts from the worship in heaven as described in Revelation 4.

### Praise
### Read Colossians 1:15-20

*Note: This is probably one of the hymns sung by Christians in the first century.*

5. In verse 15, how does Jesus Christ satisfy the person who wants to see God?

*Praying God's Words in Worship, Praise, and Confession*

6. How do verses 16 and 17 remind you of the worship scene you just studied in Revelation 4:8-11?

   What do you learn about yourself in Colossians 1:16, 17?

7. Now the focus shifts from Christ's work of creation to his work of reconciling people to God. In verse 18, what position does Christ deserve and why?

8. Describe the stupendous thing Christ accomplished in verses 19 and 20.

9. What does that accomplishment mean to you?

   Describe your relationship to God, and contrast it with what it would be if Christ had not died.

## Practicing Prayers of Praise

Speak words of praise to the Lord Jesus Christ, either for his work of creation or his work of reconciliation. You may wish simply to read this hymn as a praise to Jesus, substituting *you* and *your* for *he, him* and *his*.

*Note: In verse 19 you will need to pay attention because some of the pronouns refer to God the Father and some to Jesus his Son. Say, "For God was pleased to have all his fullness dwell in you, and through you to reconcile to himself all things."*

## Confession

An honest look at God brings us face-to-face with our own failure to be like him. He already knows all about our failures. When we agree with God, it's what he calls *confession*. In fact, the word *confession* comes from two Greek words meaning *to speak the same*, that is, *to agree*. His promise is ***if we confess our sins, he is faithful and just and will forgive us our sins and purify us from all unrighteousness*** (1 John 1:9). God's word provides a wonderful check-up opportunity.

### Read Colossians 3:1-4

10. Why should a Christian's heart and mind be focused on things above, not on things on the earth?

    How can you tell if you are obeying this command?

### Read Colossians 3:5-9

11. Some of these sins are public and obvious. Others just as ungodly, occur out of sight inside the attitude, the mind, or the privacy of personal relationships. What is God's reaction to all these sins?

12. Some of the sins listed here may be no problem for you, but others probably are. How can these verses

help the Christian who truly wants to be clean in God's sight?

## Read Colossians 3:10-17

Here the passage turns away from a list of sins to a list of godly behaviors and attitudes.

13. According to verses 10 and 11, what is the standard for a believer's behavior and attitude?

14. Of all the behaviors and attitudes listed:

   which affect your relationships (verses 11-14)?

   which affect your inner self (14-17)?

   which affect your church (15, 16)?

*Note: When we do things we shouldn't, it's called a sin of commission. When we fail to do what we should do, it's called a sin of omission. For both kinds of sin, we need God's forgiveness.*

15. Why does an unthankful person need God's forgiveness just as much as a greedy person does?

## Practicing Prayers of Confession

1. Based on your discussion of Colossians 3, some issues may have struck home as sins you need to confess to God. Do that now, either silently, or humbly trusting others in your group to hear your confession.

2. Close your time of prayer by repeating together God's wonderful promise in 1 John 1:9: *If we confess our sins, he is faithful and just and will forgive us our sins and purify us from all unrighteousness.*

## DISCUSSION 12

# Praying God's Words in Intercession and Petition

*Colossians 1:9-14; Romans 12:9-21*

God is not a cosmic order-taker at a heavenly catalog desk. We've discussed the importance of praying according to his purpose and his pattern. In Discussion 11 we learned to base prayers of worship, praise and confession on the words of God. In this study, we'll examine Bible passages to help us pray for others and ourselves. Since we can't see the deepest needs of others or even ourselves, it is wise to let God's words guide our prayers.

### Praying for Others - Intercession

*Note: The word "intercede" means to go between. When we pray for others, it's like touching them with one hand and touching God with the other.*

### Read Colossians 1:9-14

1. What three closely related things does Paul pray for his friends in verse 9?

2. Name the seven qualities that will characterize Paul's friends as God answers the prayer of verse 9:

   verse 10a

   verse 10b

   verse 10c

   verse 10d

   verse 11a

   verse 11b

   verse 12

3. Think of the needs of someone for whom you want to pray. Write each need next to the quality in Question 2 that you think gives the best long-term solution to that need. For example, someone facing a difficult challenge might need the fifth quality (verse 11a) and someone suffering pain or loss might need the sixth (verse 11b).

4. A person's greatest spiritual struggle often comes from not grasping what Jesus has already done in every believer. How can praying verses 12 and 13 for that person help meet that need?

5. Here the words *kingdom* and *dominion* refer not to a political system but to the authority or sovereign power of a ruler. Based on your recent studies on prayer, as well as your observations of life, name some contrasts between the ***dominion of darkness*** and the ***kingdom of light,*** also called ***the kingdom of the Son.***

   How does understanding these competing kingdoms affect your prayers for your friends?

6. What other benefits belong to those in the kingdom of the Son according to verse 14?

*Note: The word **Redemption** comes out of the history of slavery. It refers to paying a ransom so a slave can go free. When Paul speaks of redemption through Christ's death, he includes two concepts: paying the debt of our guilt, which would otherwise condemn us to judgment, and setting us free from sin's power to control us.*

7. How are redemption and forgiveness related?

   In what ways does redemption go beyond forgiveness?

8. How can verses 13 and 14 guide your prayers for those who don't yet know Christ as their Savior?

   How can they guide your prayers for other Christians?

## Practicing Prayers of Intercession

Take turns praying through these verses for someone you know. Be careful not to betray confidences nor to engage in gossip.

## Praying for Yourself - Petition

We have already discovered that Jesus encourages us, as loved children, to confidently ask God our Father to meet our personal needs. We can expect him to hear our petitions gladly, and to be pleased when they are based on his words.

### Read Romans 12:9-21

Not only can you pray the prayers in the Bible, but you can turn other passages such as this one into prayers.

9. If your personal needs include troubled relationships, how could verses 9 and 10 guide your petitions?

10. If you pray verse 11 for yourself, how might God rearrange your priorities and your schedule?

11. Verses 12-14 assume that you will face difficult times. If you are now in one of those times, how can these verses help shape your prayers?

*Praying God's Words in Intercession and Petition*

12. Verses 15-21 focus on relationships. Read them again, noting areas where you need God's help right now.

    How could you turn these verses into a prayer for that need?

13. How can you apply verse 21 to your present situation?

## *Practicing Prayers of Petition*

1. With your Bible open to Romans 12, pray aloud for your personal needs, letting the Scripture guide your requests.

2. Thank God for what he has done in the past and for what he will do in response to today's prayers. You might complete this sentence: "Thank you, Father, for . . ." Pray as often as you like, but only one sentence at a time.

> *Give thanks in all circumstances,*
> *for this is God's will for you in Christ Jesus*
> (1 Thessalonians 5:18).

## A Closing Word

Although you have finished these studies on prayer, you can continue, for the rest of your life, to let your daily Bible reading shape your prayers. You might find it helpful to copy the chart below and keep it with your Bible.

| God's Word | Your Prayer Response |
|---|---|
| Description of God | Worship and praise |
| Command or standard you have not met | Confession |
| Promise | Application to your need |
| Description of God's blessings | Thanksgiving |
| Behavior of people in Bible times | Commitment to follow good examples and shun bad examples |

## What Should Our Group Study Next?

We recommend the Gospel of Mark, the fast paced narrative of Jesus' life, as the first book for people new to Bible study. Follow this with the Book of Acts to see what happens to the people introduced in Mark. Then in Genesis discover the beginnings of the world and find the answers to the big questions of where we came from and why we are here.

Our repertoire of guides allows great flexibility. For groups starting with *Lenten Studies*, *They Met Jesus* is a good sequel.

### Level 101: little or no previous Bible study experience
Mark *(recommended first unit of study)* or
  The Book of Mark *(Simplified English)*
Acts, Books 1 and 2
Genesis, Books 1 and 2
Psalms/Proverbs
*Topical Studies*
Lenten Studies
Foundations for Faith
*Character Studies*
They Met Jesus
Four Men of God
Lifestyles of Faith, Books 1 and 2

> **Sequence for groups reaching people from non-Christian cultures**
> Foundations for Faith
> Genesis, Books 1 and 2
> Mark
> The Book of Mark *(Simplified English)*

### Level 201: some experience in Bible study
John, Books 1 and 2
Romans
I John/James
1 Corinthians
2 Corinthians
Philippians
Colossians

*Topical Studies*
Prayer
Treasures
Relationships
Servants of the Lord
Coping with Stress
Work – God's Gift
Celebrate

### Level 301: more experienced in Bible study
Matthew, Books 1 and 2
Galatians & Philemon
1 and 2 Peter
Hebrews
1 and 2 Thessalonians, 2 & 3 John
Isaiah
Haggai, Zechariah, Malachi
Ephesians

*Topical Studies*
Courage to Cope
Set Free

Biweekly or Monthly Groups may use topical studies or character studies.

1-800-369-0307 • www.NeighborhoodBibleStudy.org

*Prayer*

## About Neighborhood Bible Studies

**Neighborhood Bible Studies, Inc.** is a leader in the field of small group Bible studies. Since 1960, NBS has pioneered the development of Bible study groups that encourage each member to participate in the leadership of the discussion.

The mission of Neighborhood Bible Studies is to:
    Enable people to investigate the Scriptures
    Encounter God in Jesus Christ
    Mature in their faith

The vision of Neighborhood Bible Studies is to:
    Change the World
    One neighborhood at a time
    Through the study of the Bible

Publication in more than 25 languages indicates the versatility of NBS cross culturally. NBS **methods and materials** are used around the world to:
  Equip individuals for facilitating discovery Bible studies
    Serve as a resource to the church

Skilled NBS personnel provide consultation by telephone or e-mail. In some areas, they conduct workshops and seminars to train individuals, clergy, and laity in how to establish small group Bible studies in neighborhoods, churches, workplaces and specialized facilities. **Call 800-369-0307 to inquire about consultation or training.**

## About the Founders

**Marilyn Kunz and Catherine Schell, authors** of many of the NBS guides, founded Neighborhood Bible Studies and directed its work for thirty-one years. Currently other authors contribute to the series.

**The cost of your study guide has been subsidized by faithful people who give generously to NBS. For more information, visit our web site: www.NeighborhoodBibleStudy.org.**

*Prayer*

## About the Author

**Carol Wilson** studies the Bible with her neighbors and works as assistant to the director of SIM International in Charlotte, NC. She has written Bible studies for her church's women's ministries, and serves as a worship leader for conferences and church groups. She facilitates Concerts of Prayer and encourages intercession for the church around the world and for people who have not yet heard of Christ.

*Prayer*

# COMPLETE LISTING of NBS STUDY GUIDES

### Getting Started
How to Start a Neighborhood Bible Study *(handbook & video)*

### Bible Book Studies
Genesis, Book One  *Beginnings with God*
Genesis, Book Two  *The Shaping of a People*
Psalms & Proverbs  *Perspective and Wisdom for Today*
Isaiah  *God's Help Is on the Way*
Haggai, Zechariah, and Malachi  *Prophets of Hope*
Matthew, Book One  *God's Promise Fulfilled*
Matthew, Book Two  *God's Purpose Fulfilled*
Mark  *Discovering Jesus*
Luke  *Good News and Great Joy*
John, Book One  *Believe and See*
John, Book Two  *Believe and Live*
Acts, Book One  *A New Beginning*
Acts, Book Two  *Paul Sets the Pattern*
Romans  *A Reasoned Faith...A Reasonable Faith*
1 Corinthians  *Finding Answers to Life's Questions*
2 Corinthians  *The Power of Weakness*
Galatians & Philemon  *Fully Accepted by God*
Ephesians  *Living in God's Family*
Philippians  *A Message of Encouragement*
Colossians  *Staying Focused on Truth*
1 & 2 Thessalonians, 2 & 3 John, Jude  *The Coming of the Lord*
Hebrews  *Unveiling Christ*
1 & 2 Peter  *Letters to People in Trouble*
1 John & James  *Faith that Knows and Shows*

### Topical Studies
Celebrate  *Reasons for Hurrahs*
Coping with Stress  *Insights from Eight Bible Leaders*
Courage to Cope  *Uncommon Resources*
Foundations for Faith  *The Basics for Knowing God*
Lenten Studies  *Life Defeats Death*
Prayer  *Communicating with God*
Relationships  *Connected to Others: God's Plan*
Servants of the Lord  *Living by God's Agenda*
Set Free  *Leaving Negative Emotions Behind*
Treasures  *Discovering God's Riches*
Work - God's Gift  *Life-Changing Choices*

### Character Studies
Four Men of God  *Unlikely Leaders*
Lifestyles of Faith, Book One  *Choosing to Trust God*
Lifestyles of Faith, Book Two  *Choosing to Obey God*
They Met Jesus  *Life-Changing Encounters*

### Simplified English
The Book of Mark  *The Story of Jesus*

Notes

*Notes*

Notes